Pearlie... I Dream

At The Doctor's Office

Written by Yvonne Bardwell Cox   Illustrations by Stacy Johnson

AuthorHouse™
1663 Liberty Drive
Bloomington, IN 47403
www.authorhouse.com
Phone: 833-262-8899

Because of the dynamic nature of the Internet, any web addresses or links contained in this book may have changed
since publication and may no longer be valid. The views expressed in this work are solely those of the author and do
not necessarily reflect the views of the publisher, and the publisher hereby disclaims any responsibility for them.

Any people depicted in stock imagery provided by Getty Images are models,
and such images are being used for illustrative purposes only.
Certain stock imagery © Getty Images.

This book is printed on acid-free paper.

Interior Image Credit: Stacy Johnson

ISBN: 978-1-6655-7176-0 (sc)
ISBN: 978-1-6655-7177-7 (e)

Library of Congress Control Number: 2022917874

Print information available on the last page.

Published by AuthorHouse 09/27/2022

authorHOUSE®

"Commit thy works unto the Lord, and thy thoughts shall be established."
Proverbs 16:3

Acknowledgements

The thought of writing children's books has pondered my inner mind for many years. From my childhood, throughout my young adult life, I have always had a sincere love and interest to work with children with special needs. I am fortunate to have experienced and to have been offered education positions requiring teaching children with and without disabilities. Yes, I am a true Educator. Throughout my teaching career, I would often imagine different scenarios related to my childhood memories. My imagination has always been broad, yet creative and detailed. Now I am retired and still at work for children, but the Lord has instilled the books in my mind and heart that He wants me to put on paper.

I am eternally grateful to my grandmama Pearl Moore Bardwell, to whom Pearlie is named. She taught us the Word of God at night in front of a small space heater. I remember the day she taught me the Lord's Prayer. To my mother, my mama, and my friend Hattie Bardwell Pace. I love you to the moon and back. Thank you for loving and taking care of me throughout my sicknesses that I did not understand the severity of. I am truly here because of you.

I am thankful for my husband, Pastor Tommy L. Cox, for his continuous encouragement and Godly wisdom and advice. I am very grateful for my son, Michael Kelly Johnson, and my daughter-in-law Stacy Johnson who have helped to make the "Pearlie...I Dream" series come to life. The both of you are truly a team of knowledgeable and creative minds. Michael joined me in editing and handling all legalities and with Stacy's ability to edit and create mind-blowing illustrations, our triangle is complete. A special thank you to Mrs. Mable Young, for confidentially reading/editing my books and offering positive comments, when I was so reluctant to ask anyone to read what I had written.

I am sincerely grateful for this opportunity to become an Author of Children's Books.

Dedication

Special dedication in memory of all my family members who are resting in the arms of the Lord. Thank you for all my beautiful memories of a lifetime.

- My grandmother, Mrs. Pearl (Grandma Pearl) Moore Bardwell (in loving memory)

- My mother, Mrs. Hattie (Mama Hattie) Bardwell Pace

- My aunt, Mrs. Martha (Auntie Martha) Bardwell Bishop (in loving memory)

- My brother, Randolph (Doc) Bardwell (in loving memory)

- My brother, Douglas (Doug) Bardwell

- My brother, Steven (Steve) Bardwell

- My sister, Patricia Ann (Tennie) Bardwell Collier

- My sister/niece, Tonda (Lil T) Bardwell Fleming

- My first cousin, Julius (Ju Ju) Bardwell

- My first cousin, Tommy Lee Bardwell Fort (in loving memory)

- My first cousin, Leonard Smith, Jr. (in loving memory). Leonard was not living in Mississippi during this time. His inspiration and support of this book series touched the very depth of my heart.

This book series is entitled Pearlie ... I Dream. Each book is about a day in the life of Pearlie. The second Pearlie ... I Dream book "At the Doctor's Office" shares Pearlie's unusual experiences at such a young age. Not truly knowing the seriousness of her health issues, Pearlie continued with ongoing weekly treatments while learning culture and lifestyle differences. Through the mind of an innocent child, she gradually grasps an early understanding of race relations and how friendships are developed.

It is early in the morning. I am not going to school today. Mama Hattie is getting ready for work. I am ready, looking out of my window, waiting to go to the doctor's office. I have been going to see the doctor for a long time now. It seems like every week. When I am there, the days are so long. I am there from the time the sun comes up to the time the sun goes down.

3

"Are you ready yet Pearlie?" called Mama Hattie. "Yes ma'am," I answered. Mrs. C is the lady Mama Hattie goes to work with. She picks us up early in the morning in her car. They carry me to the doctor's office. We rode for a short while, then up a hill and down a long driveway. Then I see a big red brick building, F. Long Hospital. I feel a little uneasy thinking about my long day ahead. My doctor's office is down a hill right next to the hospital. Mama Hattie and I walk down the stairs to his office.

Dr. H., my doctor has a big office. One side of his office is larger than the other side. There are two doors, one to enter each side of the office. Each door has a big sign on it. The door on the front of the building says "Whites Only." The door on the side of the building says "Colored Only." I soon learned the word colored and the meaning of it.

Mama Hattie and I always walk in the direction of the "COLORED ONLY" door. As we enter, I look for my seat on the small couch. Mama Hattie goes to the window to let the nurse know I am there. She gives me a kiss goodbye and tells me to be a good girl. Then she goes to work. I am not afraid to sit in the small room alone. I have been coming here for a long time now. I think every week.

AUTO

Birds

FIN

FOOD

SPORTS

FL

9

The nurses are nice and they check on me to see if I am okay. There is a table with books on it. I have tried to read them, but the words are too hard. So, I look at the pictures from page to page to tell what the words are saying. As I turn the pages, I see birds in trees and birds flying high in the sky. Most of the books have pictures of birds and some have pictures of food that is already cooked.

I can hear the people talking on the other side of the nurses station. They laugh every now and then. I can see the top of the head of a lady and a man sitting down; they must be watching TV. I can hear the TV, but I cannot see it. I don't know what they are watching either, but it must be funny. I get up and stand by the window where the nurses are. Some are working at their desks and some are walking around with papers.

13

As I look over to the other side, I see lots of toys to play with! A girl and two boys are laughing and playing with the toys. It looks like they are having so much fun! The little girl is playing with a doll and a doll house. The little boys are playing with trucks and cars. There are lots of toys everywhere! I feel good watching them play. Now I am smiling, and I do not feel all alone.

After a while, one of the nurses calls my name. "Pearlie, Pearlie", she called. I looked around, she was standing at the door. I walked over to her. She said, "Come with me Pearlie." She leads me down a hallway to a room. I know this room; it is the same room she brings me to every week! The room has a small bed with tall legs, two chairs and lots of things Doctor H. uses.

17

I sat on the bed with my legs dancing for a long time waiting for the nurse to come back. Finally, I am so glad she came back! With a smile on her face, she asked, "Are you alright Pearlie?" I answered, "Yes, but I am getting a little cold." The nurse brings me a warm blanket and lays it on the bed beside me. While watching her, I lay on the bed and cover myself up. She does something with my doctor's things and leaves the room again.

19

I feel like the bed was made just for me. It is so comfortable. The blanket is keeping me warm. Now, I am thinking about happy times at home. My mind goes back to Grandma Pearl humming sweetly, when she has all of us children sitting around her. Before I know it, I am sleeping. I am dreaming and I know I am dreaming.

21

I am awake in my dream! I am in the big room on the other side of the nurse's station. It is the room with the TV and lots of toys everywhere. The little girl and I are playing with dolls. She knows my name! "Look Pearlie, my doll has on a pink dress", she said. I am playing with a pretty doll too. She has long dark brown hair. She has on a yellow and white dress. She has a yellow ribbon in her hair. We pretend to cook dinner for our dolls using the play stove and plates. I am having so much fun!

23

"Pearlie, Pearlie", I can hear the nurse calling me. With a big yawn I ask myself, "Where am I?". I'm back in the room on the bed with the tall legs. I open my eyes and sit up. My doctor is in the room with the nurse now. "Hello Pearlie! How are you today?" asked Doctor H. I just smiled back at him. They woke me up from a good dream. Doctor H. wants to know how I have been feeling. He always asks so many questions. He asked, "Pearlie do you get tired when you are playing outside with other children? I answered, "Yes sir, sometimes".

Doctor H. looks in my ears and has me open wide as he looks down my throat. Then he listens to my heart. He and the nurse talk quietly to each other. And before I know it, he has it in his hand, something I don't like seeing. Yes, a needle! I close my eyes tightly. I can feel Doctor H. holding my right arm. He pats it, and then it happens! I try to hold my breath until it is over. I have had this done so many times until it does not hurt anymore. Maybe I am used to it by now. Afterwards, he put something on my arm to make it feel better.

Doctor H. and his nurse leave the room again. I lay my head on the soft pillow, cover up and look out the window. I can see the sun going down. It is so pretty. It looks like a big yellow and gold ball. I have been at my doctor's office for a long time today. I wonder when Mama Hattie will come to pick me up. She dropped me off on her way to work. She will pick me up on her way home from work.

I am warm and cozy, now I am sleeping again. I am awake, but I know I am dreaming. The little girl is not with me. This time, I am at home in my room playing with my two dolls. One has dark brown hair and the other has yellow hair. Their hair is long and straight. I have a doll house for them to live in too. One has on a pretty red dress and the other has on a bright yellow dress. I am getting them ready to go to church.

Suddenly, I hear the nurse talking; she is back in the room. I am awake now. Doctor H. is in the room standing by his desk. He and the nurse are quietly talking to each other. I am listening. I sit up so I can see what they are doing. He is writing on a paper pad. There is a soft knock at the door. It's Mama Hattie! A big smile comes across my face. I am so happy to see her! Now I know it is time to go home. My doctor talks with Mama Hattie. I don't understand what he is telling her, but she does.

Mama Hattie and I leave the doctor's office. The lady she works for, Mrs. C., is waiting for us in the car. "Hello Pearlie, how was your day?" she asked. "It was okay, but long," I answered. "I hope you get to feeling better soon," she said. "Thank you," I responded. Mama Hattie and I sat in the back seat of the car. I looked out the window at the stars in the sky as we rode home.

When we got home, Mama Hattie asked me to sit so she could talk with me. She told me that she loves me so much and always prays for me. She told me why I had to go to the doctor's office so much. Mama Hattie showed me the medications that I would need to take every day. I have been taking one pill. Now I must take two more pills. Mama Hattie explained to me how important it is for me to remember to take all three pills after eating breakfast every morning.

37

Then she took a surprise from behind her back! A smile as big as the summer sun shining through the trees came across my face. It was one of the dolls from my doctor's office! The one with the dark hair! My favorite one! Mama Hattie said, "Doctor H. saw you smiling standing by the nurses' station watching the little girl playing with her." She said, "He wanted you to have her."

With a big smile, Mama Hattie said, "Doctor H. wanted me to tell you that you can bring your new friend with you when you come to his office." I could not stop smiling and kept thinking to myself, thank you so much Doctor H. for my new friend! No more lonely days in the small waiting room while I wait to see my doctor. Now I have a friend to play with at my doctor's office!

The End

Pencil and paper needed. Please do not write in your book. The answers to the questions <u>are not</u> included.

Hear It, See It, Read It, and Write It

1. What is the main idea of the story?

2. Where did this story take place?

3. Who did Pearlie ride with to see Doctor H.?

4. How did Pearlie know that the nurse was a nice lady?

5. In the doctor's waiting room, what did Pearlie do?

Pencil and paper needed. Please do not write in your book. The answers to the questions <u>are</u> included.

Hear It, See It, Read It, and Write It

1. <u>What is the main idea of the story?</u> A positive outcome from within a serious situation.

2. <u>Where did this story take place?</u> At Pearlie's doctor's office.

3. <u>Who did Pearlie ride with to see Doctor H.?</u> Mama Hattie and Mrs. C.

4. <u>How did Pearlie know that the nurse was a nice lady?</u> She smiled and took good care of her.

5. <u>When will Pearlie need t take her medicine?</u> After she eats breakfast.

About the Author

Yvonne Bardwell Cox and her husband Pastor Tommy L. Cox reside in Columbus, Mississippi. She has a blended family of sons, daughters, grandchildren, and grandchildren. She is a proud alumnus who has successfully completed educational degree status to obtain a Bachelor's in Special Education (Jackson State University, Jackson, MS), Masters in Education and an Educational Specialist in Administration and Supervision (Mississippi State University, Starkville, MS). She is a lifetime professional educator and learner, who believes in securing educational opportunities for all children. She is a retired Director (Special Education, Gifted Education and 504 Services), Education Consultant, and School Board member. She has a broad array of teaching and administrative experiences. Having worked in school districts throughout (Mississippi, Georgia, and Tennessee), her desire to author children's books is a lifetime dream come true.

"When you prepare for your future, you prepare your legacy."
Yvonne Bardwell Cox

About the Illustrator

Stacy Johnson is a creative and multi-talented artisan currently residing in Tennessee with her husband Michael K. Johnson. At the age of fifteen, Stacy discovered her love for the arts through the care and mentorship of a family-owned production company called, "Joy Art Music aka JAM". During this time, she was offered numerous opportunities in writing, illustrating, creative art design, and music. It was then that Stacy discovered an infinite love and gift for many aspects of artistic expression. Stacy studied at the Art Institute of Los Angeles, CA. She is presently refining her skills as a musical performer and recording artist in her rising girl group, The Shindellas. Her multi-talents are well demonstrated throughout her various artworks and illustrations in children's book and multimedia designs.

"Big world, little you, both great!"
Stacy Johnson